Quentin Blake The Life of Birds

Doubleday

LONDON · TORONTO · SYDNEY · AUCKLAND · JOHANNESBURG

Blake's Birds

The mother-and-daughter outfits flutter behind them – one in stripes, the other in spots. Elegant, floppy trousers, I guess in silk, billow as they walk: they are a fashionable pair. But they are also avocets, or birds very like avocets, with long, upturned bills, stepping high as waders do. That drawing (12) suggests a more precise ornithological connection than some others in this book. But although it is not easy to identify a decrepit fellow (27) as any particular species, we can still recognize that this is exactly how birds and men who have seen better times may look.

Quentin Blake's genius is to put down lines which begin with the look of birds and become a comment on the behaviour of people – and to do this while still showing the particular ways of being spruce or ruffled that go with feathers and the fluency of gesture which is human.

Looking at these drawings we become aware of how easily bird metaphors arise in common speech. We say of our fellow humans that they are all of a flutter, in a flap or flocking together. We say some are henpecked, and that others preen themselves. Even fat cats feather their nests, and parents with children too long at home want them off the twig. Maybe it is because we have two legs that the way birds strut, hop or waddle brings home to us our animal nature. Blake has pointed out that this makes it easier to draw birds as people.

A silly hen walks a slack wire with nervous bravado, a great-beaked toucan alpha male humbles his servant and a group of sad waders fish grey waters – all these birds seem to be people I have met and birds I have seen. The pictures – bigger, broader, more sombre but no less lively than his book illustrations – are the product of half a century spent bringing characters to life on the page. In *The Life of Birds* Blake follows the path of great illustrators – Grandville and Lear – and fabulists – Aesop and La Fontaine. But while Aesop and La Fontaine can make a whole species stand for a kind of human behaviour – a moral point is easier to make if all peacocks are vain and silly, all jackdaws mischievous – those characterizations, however sharp, are limiting. Blake's birds are more like novelists' characters than moralists' examples. Like Daumier, he creates individuals who are examples of, but not reduced to, types.

Those two parrots dancing, two pages back. To me they seem nervous, as though they have somehow been tricked into making fools of themselves in a competition at some parrot holiday camp. But I can also, at a pinch, see them as ageing comics doing their famous double act. I say 'seem' because without the bits of dialogue printed under the pictures which nineteenth-century artists would have supplied (or had supplied by others), and with Blake's own terse labels put at the back of the book, one is invited to speculate, to make one's own associations.

The drawings are, by turns, insidiously charming, absurdly sad and fiercely observant. My reading of the sequence runs like this:

The young are noisy. Fledglings may have arguments with parents, adolescents may mooch about but children are delightful when they learn by imitation and their glooms will pass (7–11).

Then the girls become women, and preening and keening become part of their lives (12–16).

The noisy gaggle of boys grows up. They develop personalities: sexual predator, flâneur, heavy boss, downtrodden servant, raconteur and imbiber. They visit the tailor and order lunch (17–23).

Life is a struggle. The wife quacks away, friends need comfort, funds run low and old friends just look on and note that things aren't getting better. The prospect is penury, decrepitude and life on the street (24–34).

We were so hopeful. We were artists. The young, encouraged by the old, struggled to make their mark and saw their books enter the library. But even for them creation became a chore, and all fame finally had to offer was an eminence which could do little to make one forget that the end was in sight. Yet the game goes on; the young still offer their books; exhibitions are still hung (35–43).

Life, we find, is like a tightrope. The young may dance across it waving a flower to show how easy it is, but when you become a single mother it is harder to keep your foothold. Maybe if you stand quite still it will calm you for the next step; after all, look about and you see people managing all kinds of tricks. But we get older: will we really be able to get to the heavenly bunch of flowers which should reward our balancing act? It looks a long way down from up here. Can we keep going (44–9)?

Well, we do. We head for the sea. The early pleasure of seeing footprints that tell us where we have been is followed by the later one of rolling up our trousers and paddling (50–2).

We are all voyagers: whether cheerful, or encumbered by ambitious contraptions, or with friends who are both a burden and a help. Whichever way, we are heading for an unknown destination (55–8).

Blake's birds are specific in their everyday activities – having their hair done, reading, writing, crying over old letters – but when they set off on their travels or walk their slack wires their actions become metaphors for life's vicissitudes. They suggest things – feelings about getting old, for example, about the life of art, about the insufferability of silly people and the unpleasantness of bullies. It would be foolish to try to rehearse all this precisely. Over-interpretation embarrasses the drawings and the spectator.

But one can celebrate what they achieve. Those who love drawing believe that it will live as a skill, not just as abstract handwriting, despite the confused state of its habitual companion, the art of painting. That confusion is created by, among other things, the art market, the rise of photography and explorations on the edge of meaning in which genius and nonsense nudge one another. Happily there are kinds of drawing unaffected by all that. Some have been saved by their lowly status. They make mundane things clearer than other graphic media (photography, computer graphics) are able to. This, a drawing says, is how the parts of the flat-pack fit together, how the bones of the animal are articulated, how the frock will look.

But drawing can do something more remarkable, something neither painting nor photography is good at: it can show how funny, sad, silly and odd the world is. The drawn line is saturated with the character of the draughtsman – it is like handwriting but with several extra dimensions of variability. The artist's delight and despair become legible. We learn things we knew without knowing, saw without seeing.

In Blake's case character and movement are, as it were, his prey – the thing he catches. There is pleasure in the pull and turn of his lines when they are regarded as abstract marks, but they come into their full power when the abstract handwriting begins to register as part of a living creature – a glancing eye; a jumping leg; a tentatively waving arm; an expression. A person appears on the page. Or is it a bird?

Like other masters of comic art, he can discomfort us pleasurably and amuse us painfully.

Peter Campbell

The Birds

Fledglings

9

Feminine

Male

Life and Hard Times

Arts and Letters

Tightropes

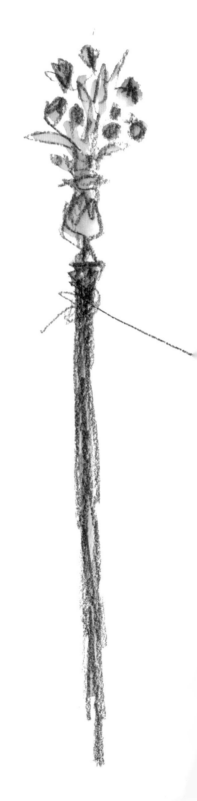

Sea and Swamp

Voyages

The Birds

1. Conversation
2. Performers

TRANSWORLD PUBLISHERS
61-63 Uxbridge Road, London W5 5SA
a division of The Random House Group Ltd

RANDOM HOUSE AUSTRALIA (PTY) LTD
20 Alfred Street, Milsons Point, Sydney,
New South Wales 2061, Australia

RANDOM HOUSE NEW ZEALAND LTD
18 Poland Road, Glenfield, Auckland 10, New Zealand

RANDOM HOUSE SOUTH AFRICA (PTY) LTD
Endulini, 5a Jubilee Road, Parktown 2193, South Africa

Published 2005 by Doubleday,
a division of Transworld Publishers,
in collaboration with the
Quentin Blake Gallery of Illustration

A catalogue record for this book is available
from the British Library.
ISBN 0385 60985X

Typeset in Adobe Caslon

Printed and bound by Mohn Media Mohndruck GmbH
1 3 5 7 9 10 8 6 4 2

Papers used by Transworld Publishers are natural, recyclable products
made from wood grown in sustainable forests. The manufacturing processes conform to the
environmental regulations of the country of origin.

The Quentin Blake GALLERY of ILLUSTRATION

Royalties from this book will go to the gallery, which will exist as a centre for illustrators and an exhibition space for past and present illustration from around the world, as well as housing Quentin Blake's archive of several thousand original drawings.